Masterpieces: Artists and Their Works

Monet

by Shelley Swanson Sateren

W
FRANKLIN WATTS
LONDON•SYDNEY

This edition first published in 2006 by

Franklin Watts   Franklin Watts Australia
338 Euston Road   Hachette Children's Books
London   Level 17/207 Kent Street
NW1 3BH   Sydney NSW 2000

ISBN-10: 0 7496 6931 4   ISBN-13: 978 0 7496 6931 7

© Capstone Press. 2002, 2004, 2006

Series created by Bridgestone Books, published by Capstone Press
151 Good Counsel Drive, P.O. Box 669, Mankato, Minnesota 56002

A CIP catalogue reference for this book is available from the British Library.

Printed in China

Consultant: Joan Lingen, Ph.D. Professor of Art History, Clarke College, Iowa, USA

Cover Art: *Detail of Water Lilies* (left) by Claude Monet and *Claude Monet* (right)
by Auguste Renoir

Editorial Credits
Blake Hoena, editor; Karen Risch, product planning editor; Heather Kindseth, cover and
interior layout designer; Katy Kudela, photo researcher

Photo Credits
Archivo Iconografico, S.A./CORBIS, cover (left); Fogg Art Museum, Harvard University
Museums, USA/Bequest from the collection of Maurice Wertheim, Class 1906/Bridgeman
Art Library, 12; Gift of Mr. and Mrs. Joseph Pulitzer/Bridgeman Library, 16; Musée des
Beaux-Arts, Nantes, France/Giraudon-Bridgeman Art Library, 20 (top); Musée Marmottan,
Paris, France/Giraudon-Bridgeman Art Library, 10; Musée d'Orsay, Paris, France/Roger-
Viollet, Paris/Bridgeman Art Library, 4; Giraudon-Bridgeman Art Library, 8, 14 (bottom);
National Gallery, London, UK/Bridgeman Art Library, 18; National Gallery of Scotland,
Edinburgh, Scotland/Bridgeman Art Library, 14 (top); Private Collection/Bridgeman Art
Library, 6; Roger-Viollet, Paris/Bridgeman Art Library, 20 (bottom); Roger-Viollet/Getty
Images, cover (right).

1 2 3 4 5 6 07 06 05 04 03 02

Table of Contents

Claude Monet is one of the most famous Impressionists.
He painted this painting, *Self Portrait*, of himself in 1917.

Claude Monet

Claude Monet (1840–1926) was a French artist. He and his artist friends invented a style of art called **Impressionism**.

Impressionists did not paint pictures that looked real. Instead, they tried to paint scenes the way they looked at a quick glance. They did this partly by using broken brush strokes.

Claude also became one of the first artists to paint mainly outdoors. For centuries, artists made rough sketches of outdoor scenes. They then painted indoors while looking at their drawings.

In his outdoor paintings, Claude showed how light and colour changed. He often painted objects in a **series**. These paintings showed the same scene at a different time of day or season. Claude is best known for his haystack series and water lily series.

Throughout his life, Claude painted many outdoor scenes. He painted *Route de Chailly, Fontainebleu* in 1864.

Young Claude

Oscar-Claude Monet was born in Paris, France, on 14th November 1840. He was the second child of Claude and Louise Monet.

When Claude was five years old, his family moved to Le Havre. This port town lies on the northern coast of France. Claude enjoyed the sea. He often watched fishermen at work and made drawings of their ships.

At the age of 14, Claude began to draw **caricatures** of well-known people in Le Havre. An art shop owner displayed these funny pictures in his store window. Claude felt proud when people began to buy his drawings.

In 1856, an artist named Eugéne Boudin visited Le Havre. He saw Claude's drawings in the shop window and was impressed by them. Eugéne invited Claude to paint with him outdoors. After spending the day painting with him, Claude knew he wanted to be an artist.

Claude asked Camille to model for *Women in the Garden*. He used her image for three of the four figures in the painting.

Paris

In 1859, Claude moved back to Paris. His aunt, Marie-Jeanne Lecadre, gave him money to study art there. In Paris, he met, studied and talked with several young artists.

Claude also met Camille Doncieux in Paris. She modelled for many of his paintings. In 1867, Claude and Camille had a son named Jean. In 1870, they married.

The Salon was a famous art gallery in Paris. Every year, it held a large art **exhibition**. Artists could submit paintings to the Salon for display.

Claude struggled to get his work accepted by the Salon, but in 1866 they accepted two of his paintings. One of the paintings was called *Women in the Garden*. The painting stood more than 2.4 metres tall. Claude created this work outdoors. He dug a trench and lowered the painting into it. He could then work on the top of the painting. Art **critics** praised Claude for these paintings.

Claude displayed *Impression, Sunrise* at an exhibition in 1874.
The word "Impressionist" was used to describe all the artists
involved in the exhibition.

Impressionism

Despite the success of 1866, it was generally difficult for Claude and his friends to get their modern art displayed at the Salon. Claude and his friends did not paint scenes that looked real, and some art critics thought their paintings were messy and child like. Many people did not understand their work.

In 1874, Claude and some other artists decided to have their own art exhibition. They wanted to show modern styles of art to the public. Artists such as Paul Cézanne, Edgar Degas and Auguste Renoir took part in this exhibition. These artists became known as Impressionists.

Impressionists wanted to capture a quick glance of the **landscapes** they painted. They painted in broken brush strokes of one solid colour. They painted different colours next to each other without mixing them. In this way, the viewer's eye could mix the colours. Impressionists' paintings look splotchy up close. But from a distance, the pictures can be seen quite clearly.

In 1877, Claude painted *The Gare Saint-Lazare: Arrival of a Train*.
Train station workers helped him by stopping trains and loading
train engines with coal to create smoke.

Struggles

In the 1870s, Claude did not sell many paintings. He often had to borrow money from friends to be able to buy food and art supplies.

In 1876, an art collector named Ernest Hoschedé hired Claude to work on some paintings. Claude became friends with the Hoschedé family and they helped him a great deal. However, by 1877, Ernest had lost most of his money and was unable to help Claude any more. Ernest also left his wife, Alice, at this time.

In 1877, Claude began to paint several works at the Saint-Lazare train station. The invention of oil paints in tubes allowed him to paint outside his studio. Before this invention, it was difficult to paint outdoors. Artists had to mix their own paints. They made paint by mixing oil with coloured substances called **pigments**. For example, an artist might have used blueberry juice to make blue paint.

Claude created many paintings of haystacks. In 1891, he painted *Haystacks: Snow Effect* (top) and *The Haystacks* (bottom) which is sometimes known as, *The End of the Summer*.

Haystacks

In 1878, Claude and Camille rented a house with Alice and her six children. That same year, Camille gave birth to her and Claude's second son, Michel.

In 1879, Camille became ill and died. It was a difficult time for Claude. His wife's death saddened him. He also struggled to sell his paintings and had very little money. However, Alice helped take care of his children so he could continue to paint.

Claude painted mostly outdoors during this time and created many paintings very quickly. He did not worry about how realistic the objects in his paintings looked. Instead, he concentrated on light and colour.

Claude painted many of the same scenes at different times of the day. He often worked for an hour or less on one painting. He then worked on another painting of the same scene when the sunlight changed. Claude's haystack paintings were done this way.

Claude often painted the cliffs near Etretat, France. This painting is titled *La Porte d'Amont, Etretat.*

Giverny

In the early 1880s, Claude began to sell more paintings. Eventually, he earned enough money to rent a house in the village of Giverny near Paris. In 1883, Alice and her children moved there with Claude and his children.

Alice agreed to take care of the children in their new home, so that Claude was able to travel. He travelled in France and other European countries and painted nature scenes wherever he went.

Claude used mostly bright colours in his paintings. He hardly mixed the paints he used. Dabs of white paint gave movement to water scenes. He also painted in broken brush strokes.

Painting outdoors was sometimes difficult for Claude. He could only work while the sun was shining. He often had to carry his art supplies through snow and down steep cliffs. One day, a large wave threw him against a cliff. He lost his art supplies and nearly drowned.

Claude owned a large water lily pond. He built a Japanese-style bridge over the pond. This painting is titled *The Water Lily Pond*.

Water Lilies

Claude planted flowers and vegetables at the house in Giverny. He enjoyed gardening and often created paintings of his gardens.

By the late 1880s, Claude had sold enough paintings to buy the house at Giverny. He then hired workers to take care of his gardens.

In 1891, Alice's husband, Ernest, died. In 1892, Claude and Alice married. After their marriage, Claude usually painted close to home. He often painted from sunrise until supper time.

In the early 1900s, Claude painted his water lily pond hundreds of times. In 1916, he began a series of huge water lily paintings. Some of these paintings were more than 3.1 metres wide.

When Claude finished his large water lily paintings, he refused to sell them. They were still hanging in his studio when he died, on 5th December 1926. Claude was 86 years old.

Claude painted many large water lily paintings. He painted *Water Lilies at Giverny* (top) in 1917.

Monet's Paintings Today

Claude's huge water lily paintings now hang in two rooms at *Le Musée de l'Orangerie* (the Orangerie Museum) in Paris. Years ago, the king of France used these two oval rooms as a greenhouse. The art museum hung the paintings there the year after Claude died.

After Claude's death, his youngest son, Michel, inherited the house at Giverny. Michel also received his father's unsold paintings. When Michel died, he left his father's paintings to *Le Musée Marmottan* (the Marmottan Museum) in Paris. The house and gardens at Giverny became a museum. Thousands of people visit them every year.

In the 1990s, the largest Monet exhibition ever held toured around the world. The organisers had gathered 159 of his paintings and thousands of people travelled to different countries to see them.

Today, art museums in Paris and Boston own large collections of Claude's paintings. Galleries in London, Cardiff and Edinburgh also have collections of his art.

Timeline

1840 – Claude is born on 14th November.

1856 – Eugene Boudin visits Le Havre and meets Claude.

1859 – Claude moves to Paris to study art.

1866 – Claude has two of his paintings accepted at the Salon.

1867 – Claude's first son, Jean, is born.

1870 – Claude marries Camille Doncieux.

1874 – Claude takes part in the first Impressionist exhibition.

1878 – Claude's second son, Michel, is born.

1879 – Camille dies.

1883 – Claude rents the house at Giverny.

1892 – Claude marries Alice Hoschedé.

1911 – Alice dies.

1914 – World War I (1914–1918) begins; Jean dies later in the war.

1926 – Claude dies at Giverny on 5th December.

Useful Websites

www.giverny.org/monet/
As the 'official' Monet website, this site explores his paintings and shows photographs of his house and gardens at Giverny. It also contains details of Monet books, museums showing his work and the latest Monet exhibitions around the world.

www.expo-monet.com
This website displays a large collection of Monet's paintings. Specific paintings can be searched for by title, theme, year, style or keywords.

www.bbc.co.uk/arts/
impressionism/
The BBC's website includes lots of information about Monet and other Impressionists. Contains activities such as step-by-step guides to creating your own Impressionist painting.

www.biblio.org/wm/auth/monet/
This detailed website contains a biography and a large selection of paintings, grouped chronologically.

www.whytownps.sa.edu.au/
visarts/
This Australian school website looks at many different artists, including Impressionists, and explores their various styles of art. It also provides a range of art activities and quizzes.

Note to parents and teachers
Every effort has been made by the Publishers to ensure that these websites are suitable for children; that they are of the highest educational value, and that they contain no inappropriate or offensive material. However, because of the nature of the Internet, it is impossible to guarantee that the contents of these sites will not be altered. We strongly advise that Internet access is supervised by a responsible adult.

Glossary

caricature – an exaggerated, funny drawing of someone
critic – someone who reviews art, books, or films
exhibition – a public display that people visit
Impressionism – an art style in which broken brush strokes are used to paint a scene the way it looks at a quick glance
Impressionists – artists who use the style of Impressionism
landscape – a piece of artwork of an outdoor scene
pigment – a coloured substance artists used to make paint
series – a number of pieces of art about the same subject

Index